Winning the War
Through Prayer

Tina Ogundiran

And pray in the Spirit on all occasions with all kinds of prayers and requests. With this in mind, be alert and always keep on praying for all the Lord's people.

- Ephesians 6:18 (NIV)

TABLE OF CONTENTS

- Pray without Cease
- Pray the Word
- Pray with Faith

A NOTE TO THE READER

If you're reading this book, chances are you've recognized the season we're in. We are at war. From racial division, to political and social extremes, and the growing number of social injustices. The world is not without its issues. And, these are just those that are happening outside the home. What about everything going on behind our closed doors?

This question begs us all to take a look at our surroundings, at our circumstances and accept that there is war there too. We aren't being as selfless as we need to be. There are trust issues in our relationships. Perhaps, the bills are plenty and the funds are few. Maybe we've strayed away from our spiritual teachings. Whatever the disarray, it's important that we all understand that there is help.

We don't have to fight the wars alone. And, they can be won, if we learn to pray.

This book is my gift to you. A guide, of sorts, of things that I've learned throughout my journey about the war we're in and how it can be won through prayer. If you are struggling with anything in your life, with your family or in your ministry, this book is for you. Allow it to aid you as you walk and live in total victory, providing for you the tools you will need to win the war.

War *DEFINED*

War, as defined by Webster's Dictionary, *is a conflict carried on by force of arms, as between nations or between parties within a nation; warfare, as by land, sea, or air or a state or period of armed hostility or active military operations.* Webster simplifies war; it presents the idea that war is in the physical only, with its forces of arms between nations. But reality has shown us that there is a second kind of war: the spiritual.

We all are well aware of what a physical war is. Take for instance the American Civil War. A war fought in the United States from 1861 to 1865 over slavery and state rights. It resulted in over 600,000 people dead, the dissolution of the confederate states, the abolishment of slavery, and the beginning of the reconstruction era. The war required human effort, and the support of weapons.

No one really *wants* to go to war, but in many cases, it's necessary to achieve a specific result. Wars differ in their interests, their objectives; they also differ in the manpower required to produce a favorable outcome.

On the flip side of the same coin is spiritual war or warfare. This is the war that exists between Christians and Satan's team of evil doers. And, quite frankly, it takes strategy and intentional effort to stand against the schemes that Satan casts in the life of a believer on a daily basis.

Spiritual warfare doesn't get a lot of press. Instead it's felt in the lives of believers at the hand of Satan's team, who are spiritual beings. They are not subject to human sensory and are above the operation of natural law. However, just because we don't see them doesn't mean they don't exist.

Wherein in time past ye walked according to the course of this world, according to the prince of the power of the air, the spirit that now worketh in the children of disobedience (Ephesians 2:2, NIV).

Sometimes we overlook the presence of Satan, because he doesn't live next door or greet us in the supermarket. *"Do not I fill heaven and earth?"* *declares the Lord* (Jeremiah 23:24, NIV). Just as God is everywhere, so is Satan. Even more reason for us to arm ourselves.

Finally, be strong in the Lord and the strength of his might. Put on the whole armor of God, so that you can take your stand against the devil's schemes. For our struggle is not against flesh and blood, but against the rulers, against the authorities, against the powers of this dark world and against the spiritual forces of evil in the heavenly realms.

Therefore, put on the full armor of God, so that when the day of evil comes, you may be able to stand your ground, and after you have done everything, to stand. Stand firm then, with the belt of truth buckled around your waist, with the breastplate of righteousness in place, and with your feet fitted with the readiness that comes from the gospel of peace.

In addition to all this, take up the shield of faith, with which you can extinguish all the flaming arrows of the evil one. Take the helmet of salvation and the sword of the Spirit, which is the word of God. And pray in the Spirit on all occasions with all kinds of prayers and requests. with this in mind, be alert and always keep on praying for all the Lord's people (Ephesians 6:10-18).

In understanding war, we must acknowledge that spiritual warfare exists for us all. And, that it continues whether we believe it to be so or not. As we get further from biblical times, and the traditions of our forefathers fade away, we start to notice people taking these things less and less seriously. People begin to question more and trust faithfully a little less. However, the line is still clear. We are either a victor or victim.

When Jesus hung his head and died, he did so, so that we might have everlasting life. Through him. And, by his grace. *Then Jesus came to them and said, "All authority in heaven and on earth has been given to me. Therefore, go and make disciples of all nations, baptizing them in the name of the Father and of the Son and of the Holy Spirit, and teaching them to obey everything I have commanded you. And surely, I am with you always, to the very end of the age* (Matthew 28:18-20, NIV)."

Everlasting life is achieved by staying strong in the spiritual warfare that we experience in our lives every day. Our strength is shown in our constant, consistent, and intentional communication with the Lord. We are strong by believing in his word, and sharing it with others.

Spiritual warfare isn't some *hyperbolized* thing, despite our inability to see Satan and his team, they are there, giving us reason after reason to succumb. But, there is hope. And, accepting that the war exists is step one.

War's *PURPOSE*

The fall of man marked the beginning of spiritual warfare, as Adam disobeyed God's commandment and ate of the fruit, alongside Eve. *But the serpent said to the woman, "You will not certainly die. For God knows that when you eat from it your eyes will be opened, and you will be like God, knowing good and evil"* (Genesis 3:4-5, NIV). See here how Satan influenced Eve to believe that what God told Adam was wrong. That, they wouldn't die; instead they would have knowledge.

Often times Satan will influence our thoughts, and have us second guessing what God has told us to be truth. We must stand firmly in His word otherwise, we will lose the war. Although Adam and Eve did not immediately die, they both would physically die in their lifetime. And, all of us are destined to do the same. *For you are dust,* and to dust you shall return" (Genesis 3:19, NIV).

So, what is the purpose of spiritual warfare? *The one who does what is sinful is of the devil, because the devil has been sinning from the beginning. The reason the Son of God appeared was to destroy the devil's work* (I John 3:8, NIV). What we know is that Satan has always been evil, God manifested himself in human form to defeat him. *In the beginning was the Word, and the Word was with God, and the Word was God* (John 1:1, NIV). *The Word became flesh and made his dwelling among us. We have seen his glory, the glory of the one and only Son, who came from the Father, full of grace and truth* (John 1:14, NIV).

Who gave himself for our sins to rescue us from the present evil age, according to the will of our God and Father (Galatians 1:4, NIV). Jesus paid the ultimate price, so that we may have everlasting life. *For God so loved the world that he gave his one and only Son, that whoever believes in him shall not perish but have eternal life* (John 3:16, NIV). Spiritual warfare is a test. Similar to Eve in the garden, we will be tempted but we must hold on to the Lord's unchanging hand. The bible reads: *Jesus Christ is the same yesterday and today and forever* (Hebrews 13:8, NIV). Can you resist temptation?

History will culminate with the defeat of Satan. *He seized the dragon, that ancient serpent, who is the devil, or Satan, and bound him for a thousand years* (Revelations 20:2, NIV). *When the thousand years are over, Satan will be released from his prison and will go out to deceive the nations in the four corners of the earth—Gog and Magog—and to gather them for battle. In number, they are like the sand on the seashore.*

They marched across the breadth of the earth and surrounded the camp of God's people, the city he loves. But fire came down from heaven and devoured them. And the devil, who deceived them, was thrown into the lake of burning sulfur, where the beast and the false prophet had been thrown. They will be tormented day and night for ever and ever (Revelations 20:7-10, NIV).

Satan and his demons realize there is no fellowship between light and darkness. *When he saw Jesus, he cried out and fell at his feet, shouting at the top of his voice, "What do you want with me, Jesus, Son of the most-high God? I beg you, don't torture me"* (Luke 8:28, NIV)! And, they entreat favor from Christ. *And they begged Jesus repeatedly not to order them to go into the Abyss* (Luke 8:31, NIV).

They understand the future and their own doom. *But the subjects of the kingdom will be thrown outside, into the darkness, where there will be weeping and gnashing of teeth* (Matthew 8:12, NIV).

This war is a battle for 3 things: your position, power, and promises. Your position is where you as a believer stand in your relationship with Christ. *And God raised us up with Christ and seated us with him in the heavenly realms in Christ Jesus* (Ephesians 2:6, NIV). *This is how love is made complete among us so that we will have confidence on the day of judgment: In this world, we are like Jesus* (I John 4:17, NIV). *Since, then, you have been raised with Christ, set your hearts on things above, where Christ is, seated at the right hand of God* (Colossians 3:1, NIV). *But our citizenship is in heaven. And we eagerly await a Savior from there, the Lord Jesus Christ* (Philippians 3:20, NIV).

Satan is after your position. Your position is a sign that you are connected to God. He lost his position with God, the bible denotes this in Isaiah 14:2-17. He is jealous of your position and wants to push you further away from God. Consider Matthew 4:1-11, when Jesus is tested in the Wilderness.

Jesus Christ, the mighty warrior, is challenged to give in and join Satan. Observe how Jesus Christ won the battle over Satan. Each temptation was defeated with the word of God. *After fasting forty days and forty nights, he was hungry. The tempter came to him and said, "If you are the Son of God, tell these stones to become bread." Jesus answered, "It is written: 'Man shall not live on bread alone, but on every word, that comes from the mouth of God'* (Matthew 4:2-4, NIV).

In Job, Satan is convinced that Job will leave his position with God over the loss of a possessions. *But now stretch out your hand and strike everything he has, and he will surely curse you to your face* (Job 1:11, NIV). What he failed to realize was that God had already qualified Job for the test. God knew Job loved him, and that he would strive to maintain his position with God.

He passed and was rewarded greatly for not giving up his place with God. We are in a good place of favor and victory. We are loved by our heavenly Father and must continue to stay in that position where all that he is works in and through us.

Satan is also after our Power. *When Jesus had called the Twelve together, he gave them power and authority to drive out all demons and to cure diseases, and he sent them out to proclaim the kingdom of God and to heal the sick* (Luke 9:1-2, NIV). We have been given power over Satan and his demons to shut down demonic activity. *I have given you authority to trample on snakes and scorpions and to overcome all the power of the enemy; nothing will harm you* (Luke 10:19, NIV).

Lastly, this war is to rob us of our promises from God. Having a relationship with God has its rewards. *His divine power has given us everything we need for a godly life through our knowledge of him who called us by his own glory and goodness*

(II Peter 1:3, NIV). We gain access through him; by getting to know him, understanding His word, and speaking with him consistently and intentionally. *Praise be to the God and Father of our Lord Jesus Christ, who has blessed us in the heavenly realms with every spiritual blessing in Christ* (Ephesians 1:3, NIV).

God doesn't wish for us to struggle; he doesn't want us to lack, worry about tomorrow, or stress over sickness. His son took it all to the cross making it possible for us to live in victory. We have an inheritance, and we should commit ourselves to keeping it, even if that means war.

Prayer *DEFINED*

Prayer is an act of communion with God; it is devotion, confession, praise, and thanksgiving. Prayer is speaking with God, and it isn't one-sided. We must also listen to hear what he says in return. A common misconception is that prayer is a monologue. It is actually dialogue because God talks back.

The first mention of prayer in the Bible: *Seth also had a son, and he named him Enosh. At that time, people began to call on the name of the Lord.* (Genesis 4:26, NIV). There were conversations that existed before this verse however, the very distinct difference is that, previously, they were all initiated by God.

We see prayer in action in Genesis where Adam and Eve had the privilege to freely converse with God on a daily basis. After the fall of man, there was a shift. In Genesis 4:26, many developed the desire to speak with God; it was at that time that people began to call on the name of the Lord.

Calling on the Lord symbolized the line that was being drawn in the sand between good and evil. After the fall of humanity, it took time, but people began to realize they could not walk alone. So, they looked to the Lord for guidance. Prayer is one of the oldest weapons against evil. It is our life line in a state of emergency.

There isn't a single type, nor is there a specific prayer. Instead, there are types of prayer that we can use to guide our conversation with the Lord. Let's take a look at the various types.

The Prayer of Faith – *And the prayer offered in faith will make the sick person well; the Lord will raise them up. If they have sinned, they will be forgiven* (James 5:15, NIV). This type of prayer is two-fold, it says that we can pray for sickness *but* we must have faith that what we pray will come to pass. *If you can, said Jesus. "Everything is possible for one who believes* (Mark 9:23, NIV)."

The Prayer of Agreement - *They all joined together constantly in prayer, along with the women and Mary the mother of Jesus, and with his brothers* (Acts 1:14, NIV). As the name states, this prayer is in agreement, it is meant to edify and unify those who take part. Often times we seclude ourselves, thinking it's best to do so. When the word states the exact opposite. By taking your burdens to the group, you will be encouraged and uplifted by those praying on your behalf.

The Prayer of Supplication – We should take our requests to God. *Do not be anxious about anything, but in every situation, by prayer and petition, with thanksgiving, present your requests to God.* (Philippians 4:6, NIV). Winning the war takes prayer at all times.

The Prayer of Thanksgiving – *I will praise God's name in song and glorify him with thanksgiving* (Psalms 69:30, NIV). This type of communication with God is giving thanks. *Enter his gates with thanksgiving and his courts with praise; give thanks to him and praise his name* (Psalms 100:4, NIV).

The Prayer of Worship – This prayer type is also thankful to God however, in this case, it is because of who is he is and not just what he's done. *Then the man bowed down and worshipped the Lord* (Genesis 24:26, NIV).

The Prayer of Consecration — Sometimes, life calls us to be greater than we are. And, in such cases we must pray for God's will to be done. *Going a little farther, he fell with his face to the ground and prayed, "My Father, if it is possible, may this cup be taken from me. Yet not as I will, but as you will* (Matthew 26:39, NIV). This prayer comes just before crucifixion. The shoes may be big to fill, we may wish that the responsibility fell on another, but alas, if it is God's will, then it will be done.

The Prayer of Intercession — To intercede is to intervene on the behalf of another. *Therefore, I will give him a portion among the great, and he will divide the spoils with the strong; because he poured out his life unto death, and was numbered with the transgressors. For he bore the sin of many, and made intercession for the transgressors* (Isaiah

53:12 NIV). *Therefore, he is able to save completely those who come to God through him, because he always lives to intercede for them* (Hebrews 7:25, NIV).

The Prayer of Imprecation – This prayer type is mentioned last on purpose, because the Bible teaches us that we should not curse or speak ill of our enemies. *But I tell you, love your enemies and pray for those who persecute you* (Matthew 5:44, NIV). However, the prayer of imprecation is seen in the book of Psalms. Not intentionally to curse, instead to emphasize that God is just and will cast judgment on those who are evil, and not living in accordance with His will.

Now that you have a better understanding on how to communicate with God, it is my hope that you can continue this book with a prepared and open

mind to receive the tools to win the war in your life.

Prayer's *PURPOSE*

As a minister and a believer in His word, praying is second nature for me. However, I know that not everyone feels the same comfort when communicating with God.

When I've asked believers *why don't they pray,* I've received responses that ranged from not knowing how, to feeling like they needed a *gift* of prayer, and even feeling as though they were better suited having someone pray on their behalf.

Some have even attested to being too tired. They've had a long day at work, and once they get home, their second job commences with taking care of the home. And, in many cases, it isn't priority and falls victim to the *I don't have time* rhetoric.

To them I respond, it's not about having time, instead it's about making time. Here's the thing, prayer is not a hobby. It's a lifestyle. It is us giving

God the permission to get involved in our lives. And, once you change the way you view the act of prayer, the reasons why you should pray will become clearer.

The Bible teaches us that we must pray without cease. *Rejoice always, pray continually, give thanks in all circumstances; for this is God's will for you in Christ Jesus* (Thessalonians 5:16-18, NIV). And, we learn that in our consistent and continual prayer, God will make a way when there seems to be no way. *This is what the Lord says – he who made a way through the sea, a path through the mighty waters* (Isaiah 43:16, NIV).

Who can make a path through sea? Our sense tells us this is impossible. That water, itself, is continual and cannot be split. And, in that is what we must realize and recognize about the Lord. He is all powerful. The things that seem hopeless in our eyes and by our logic are nothing for him. The things that seem impossible are possible through him. The Lord will even use those who don't believe to do his work on your behalf.

Then Jesus told his disciples a parable to show them that they should always pray and not give up. He said: "In a certain town there was a judge who neither feared God nor cared what people thought. And there was a widow in that town who kept coming to him with the plea, 'Grant me justice against my adversary (Luke 18:1-3, NIV).'

"For some time. he refused. But finally, he said to himself, 'Even though I don't fear God or care what people think, yet because this widow keeps bothering me, I will see that she gets justice, so that

she won't eventually come and attack me (Luke 18: 4-5, NIV)!"

And the Lord said, "Listen to what the unjust judge says. And will not God bring about justice for his chosen ones, who cry out to him day and night? Will he keep putting them off? I tell you, he will see that they get justice, and quickly. However, when the Son of Man comes, will he find faith on the earth (Luke 18:6-8, NIV)?"

What we see here is a testament to the faithfulness of God in response to our faithfulness in prayer. He used a man who didn't fear him, who had no regard for people to do his will. That's his power. It is also proof of the power in prayer. And, it should serve as reason enough to make the time to speak with God.

Satan will have you thinking that you are too busy. He will lead you to believe that prayer isn't important. That you can do it later. That God knows your heart, and that alone is enough. It isn't. We are commanded to pray. *Do not be anxious about anything, but in every situation, by prayer and petition, with thanksgiving, present your requests to God. And the peace of God, which transcends all understanding, will guard your hearts and your minds in Christ Jesus* (Philippians 4:6-7, NIV).

Let us not confuse our prayer with the carrying out of our own will, instead it is the will of God. When we pray for things that are in accordance with his will, the word says that it will come to pass. *This is the confidence we have in approaching God: that if we ask anything according to his will, he hears us. And if we know that he hears us—whatever we ask—we know that we have what we asked of him* (I John 5:14-15, NIV).

Yet another reason why speaking with God is so important. The more we communicate with him, the more we immerse ourselves in his word, the more clarity we will have in understanding God's will. *Therefore, I urge you, brothers and sisters, in view of God's mercy, to offer your bodies as a living sacrifice, holy and pleasing to God—this is your true and proper worship. Do not conform to the pattern of this world, but be transformed by the renewing of your mind. Then you will be able to test and approve what God's will is—his good, pleasing and perfect will* (Romans 12:1-2, NIV). The more closely we follow God, the clearer it will be.

The Bible teaches us what God wants: *Rejoice always, pray continually, give thanks in all circumstances; for this is God's will for you in Christ Jesus* (I Thessalonians 5:16-18, NIV). He wants us to be joyful. To communicate with him consistently and intentionally. And, to be thankful. And, as wars rage all around us, we can stand in comfort knowing that *the grace of our Lord Jesus Christ be with you* (I Thessalonians 5:28, NIV). Simply because we understand prayer and the value it has in our lives.

Winning the *WAR*

Pray without Ceasing

One of the first lines of defense in winning the war in your life is to maintain a praying spirit. Satan wants you to doubt God. He wants you to second guess the things that the Father has made clear. Research shows us that mental attacks are among the lethal. They rob you of your comfort, of your esteem, and your peace. Once you've been attacked mentally, it becomes easy to shake the other areas of your life. However, with constant and consistent prayer, you are equipped to defeat Satan. *The thief comes only to steal and kill and destroy; I have come that they may have life, and have it to the full* (John 10:10, NIV).

Be joyful in hope, patient in affliction, faithful in prayer (Romans 12:12, NIV). The dictionary defines hope as something we want to happen. God wants us to be joyful in our hopes. Our reality is that as followers of Christ, we will experience trials and tribulations. However, *let us not become weary in doing good, for at the proper time we will reap the harvest if we do not give up* (Galatians 6:9). And, that's in the midst of the attacks on our minds, of our spirits, and in some cases, our physical being. We must remain joyful, and steadfast in our prayers with God.

In the midst of our afflictions, we must be patient. *The righteous cry out, and the Lord hears them; he delivers them from their troubles. The Lord is close to the brokenhearted and saves those who are crushed in spirit. The righteous people may have many troubles, but the Lord delivers him from them all; he protects all his bones, not one of them will be broken* (Psalms 34:17-20, NIV). Satan wants us to live in fear, tearing from us every ounce of peace. But the Bible teaches us, *so do not fear, for I am with you; do not be dismayed, for I am your God. I will strengthen you and help you; I will uphold you with my righteous right hand* (Isaiah 41:10, NIV).

Pray the Word

As we strengthen our bond with God, we must remember to pray the word. Matthew 6:9-13 give us a great starting point with the Lord's Prayer. It provides a foundation for our communication with God, and a place from which to base our own private moments with the Lord. It affirms to whom we pray, it recognizes from where our help comes, how imperfect we are in our daily lives and how forgiving he is in spite of.

The word teaches us that God hears our prayers. *This is the confidence we have in approaching God: that if we ask anything according to his will, he hears us* (I John 5:14, NIV). Not only is it important to pray the word, it is important to know the word. In it lies the answers that we seek. *So is my word that goes out of my mouth: it will not return to me empty, but will accomplish what I desire and achieve the purpose for which I sent it* (Isaiah 55:11, NIV).

The word gives us the armor we need. It gives us wisdom. *The unfolding of your words gives light; it gives understanding to the simple* (Psalms 119:130, NIV). It guides our steps. *Your word is a lamp to my feet, a light on my path* (Psalms 119:105, NIV). It removes the weight of the trials. *My soul is weary with sorrow; strengthen me according to your word* (Psalms 119:28, NIV). It gives us peace amid the storm. *Great peace have those who love your law, and nothing can make them stumble* (Psalms 119:165, NIV). All of which is necessary as we fight this war.

Pray with Faith

We must continually pray, know and speak the word, and do so with faith. *Who is it that overcomes the world? Only the ones who believes that Jesus is the Son of God* (I John 5:5, NIV). I hear all too often how difficult it is to remain faithful, but I urge you to do so. *He replied, "because you have so little faith. Truly I tell you, if you have faith the size of a mustard seed, you can say to this mountain, move from here to there, and it will move. Nothing will be impossible for you* (Matthew 17:20, NIV).

Everything you're dealing with, every battle you face, every war you experience can be won with the belief that it can be done. *For God so loved the world that he gave his one and only Son, that whoever believes in him shall not perish but have eternal life* (John 3:16, NIV). God wants to see you win, he doesn't want you to be defeated. But, you must understand the power in faith. *But when you ask, you must believe and not doubt, because the one who doubts is like the wave of the sea, blown and tossed by the wind* (James 1:6, NIV).

Your prayers will not return to you void, God is listening. *You will pray to him, and he will hear you, and you will fulfill your vows* (Job 22:27, NIV). And, he is able to go above and beyond what we ask of him. *Therefore, I tell you, whatever you ask in prayer, believe that you have received it, and it will be yours* (Mark 11:24, NIV).

Conclusion

It is my belief that all of our purposes are wrapped up in people. That, in large part, is why I felt compelled to write this book. I encounter countless people who feel lost, who want to pray and connect with God but they just don't know where to start. And, well, I have taken it upon myself to be the light.

I want this book to serve as a tool to guide them a little closer to Jesus, because I truly believe, just as the bible says, that *he is the way and the truth and the life. No one comes to the Father except through the son* (John 14:6, NIV). If my words help your journey in even the slightest way, then I have served my purpose.

We all face wars, that's just the reality of those of us who follow Christ. But now you have an understanding of spiritual warfare and its purpose, it's time for you to be a little more intentional in how you defeat the enemy.

It is Satan's goal to steal, kill, and destroy, but you don't have to be destroyed. God doesn't want that as your fate. Instead, he wants you to have life everlasting. And, the way to have it is through him and his son, Jesus.

In these days and times, it's important that we have an in depth understanding of the word. Our connections to God is not defined by how loud we are or how flashy we dress, it is a direct reflection of the work we put in to be humble servants of his word, his teachings.

I pray that this book may bless your life, your season, and your work. Remember, you are not alone. *One thing God has spoken, two things I have heard: Power belongs to you, God, and with you,*

Lord, is unfailing love, and you reward everyone according to what they have done (Psalms 62:11-12, NIV).

Self-*STUDY*

1. Can you identify the war(s) in your life?

2. Up to this point, what has been your strategy for winning the war(s) in your life?

3. Do you feel you are in this battle alone? Who is fighting with you?

4. What can you learn from the war(s) taking place in your life?

5. How often do you pray?

6. Is your prayer consistent?

7. Do you pray intentionally?

8. How great is your belief that God is listening and will act on your behalf?

9. Do you study the word so that you can pray the word?

10. When your faith is tested, do you find it difficult to let go and let God?

11. Do you surround yourself with a community of believers?

12. After reading this book, what improvements can be made in your life to better prepare you for spiritual warfare?

NOTES

ACKNOWLEDGEMENTS

First and foremost, I would like to give honor to God, who is the head of my life. His immeasurable grace is why I am able to write his goodness. I am a living testimony that prayer is the ultimate armor in winning the war. I am forever grateful for the ultimate sacrifice.

To my husband, I express my deepest appreciation. You have been a loyal supporter and motivator. Thank you for covering me in prayer. Whatever I've wanted to do, you have been there to push me and you've helped me with everything I've needed.

To my church family, Ever Changing Lives Ministry and our partners, you all have been a big support. I can't thank you enough for the overflow of love, support and prayers throughout this project.

To my mentor, Mrs. Wanda Casey, thank you for being an inspiration to me over the years. I will be forever indebted to you for encouraging me to take this leap of faith. It was your push that helped me turn my ministry into a project that people across the world can access.

To my Spiritual Parents and our overseers, Bishop Malverse and Lady Rosaline Simpson, thank you for taking me in as a daughter and for investing so much in me. I am grateful for having you as my teachers, teaching me how to pray and its importance. Because of you, I have a strong foundation from which to pull my message.

Special thanks to Laneshia Lamb, the writer-who was able to bring my message to life. I appreciate the work you've done on this project, the patience you've had, and the time you've invested to ensure the project was exactly what I wanted it to be.

Last, but certainly not least, to my readers, thank you for your support, for your openness in your personal journey, and for seeking God in winning the wars in your life.

ABOUT THE AUTHOR

Evangelist, Tina Ogundiran, was born in Bedford, Virginia, where she lived until she was 25; she then relocated to Roanoke, Virginia. A 2002 graduate of Liberty University College in Lynchburg, Virginia, Tina completed her studies at the Biblical Institution. She later completed her ministerial studies at the Spirit Led Bible Institution in Roanoke, Virginia.

Tina became licensed in 2003 as an Evangelist under Spirit of Liberty Worship Center. In 2010, under the guidance of the Holy Spirit, she transferred to Greensboro, NC where she currently lives with her husband. She has been involved in ministry for over seventeen years and is the Co-founder of Ever Changing Lives Ministry in Greensboro North Carolina.

Co-Pastor, Ogundiran, is a dedicated worker in the Kingdom and has been preaching the gospel of Jesus for seventeen years. In her earlier years, she developed a love and passion for prayer. She became a strong intercessor in her local church resulting in her being ushered into teaching the principles of prayer. Her experiences have created a path for her as a speaker. She is a well-known general in the Body of Christ when it comes to understanding prayer, she even has a prayer line that touches people worldwide.

Tina operates in deliverance and healing; has a strong prophetic anointing. She truly loves God's people. Evangelist Tina Ogundiran believes that with God all things are possible to them that believe if we only pray.